Table of Contents

Chapter 1

GEOGRAPHY AND CLIMATE

Kenya is a nation of beauty and diversity. From its coastline along the Indian Ocean to its towering highlands, Kenya is home to vibrant cultures, a wide range of wildlife, and a rich history.

The Land

Kenya is in East Africa. It covers 224,081 square miles (580,367 sq. km). It is the fifty-first-largest country in the world. Kenya borders the Indian Ocean, Tanzania, Uganda,

Searchlight
BOOKS™

World Traveler

Travel to

Kenya

Matt Doeden

Lerner Publications ◆ Minneapolis

Content consultant: Dr. Mumbi Mwangi, professor of Gender and Women's Studies at
Saint Cloud State University, Saint Cloud, Minnesota

Lerner Publications Company
An imprint of Lerner Publishing Group, Inc.
241 First Avenue North
Minneapolis, MN 55401 USA

For reading levels and more information, look up this title
at www.lernerbooks.com.

Main body text set in Adrianna Regular.
Typeface provided by Chank.

Designer: Mary Ross

Library of Congress Cataloging-in-Publication Data

Names: Doeden, Matt author.
Title: Travel to Kenya / Matt Doeden.
Description: Minneapolis : Lerner Publications , [2022] | Series: Searchlight Books —
    World Traveler | Includes bibliographical references and index. | Audience: Ages
    8–11 years | Audience: Grades 4–6 | Summary: "Kenya is an East African country
    with an exciting variety of cultures and wildlife. Follow along as we explore Kenya's
    landscape, with topics ranging from life in the city to beautiful highlands and
    valleys"— Provided by publisher.
Identifiers: LCCN 2021022709 (print) | LCCN 2021022710
    (ebook) | ISBN 9781728441658 (Library Binding) | ISBN 9781728448848 (Paperback) |
    ISBN 9781728445021 (eBook)
Subjects: LCSH: Kenya—Description and travel—Juvenile literature. | Kenya—History. |
    Geography—Kenya. | Kenya—Social life and customs.
Classification: LCC DT433.527 .D64 2022 (print) | LCC DT433.527 (ebook) | DDC
    916.76204—dc23

LC record available at https://lccn.loc.gov/2021022709
LC ebook record available at https://lccn.loc.gov/2021022710

Manufactured in the United States of America
1-49920-49763-9/3/2021

South Sudan, Ethiopia, and Somalia. From its coastline, a low plain rises to the country's central highlands. The Great Rift Valley, a large ridge, splits the highlands. The valley sits where two of Earth's tectonic plates are pulling apart. Scientists believe the valley is tearing the land in two.

Tsavo West National Park, Kenya

East of the Great Rift Valley is a highland plateau. Mount Kenya rises there. It is the nation's highest point. The mountain is 17,057 feet (5,199 m) above sea level.

Rivers and Lakes

Many rivers run through Kenya. The longest is the Tana River. It flows for 440 miles (708 km). Then it empties into the Indian Ocean. Along its way, it tumbles over the Kitaru Falls. The falls is popular with tourists. Other important Kenyan rivers include the Ewaso Ng'iro and the Dawa River.

The banks of the Tana River are busy. Goats drink and people wash their clothes and launch canoes.

ON THE MAIN BEACH AT LAKE VICTORIA, FISHERS SELL OMENA. THESE ARE SMALL, SARDINELIKE FISH.

Part of Lake Victoria crosses over Kenya's western border. It is Africa's largest lake. Most people consider it the source of the Nile River. Lake Turkana is the largest desert lake in the world. This saltwater lake lies in Kenya.

Palm trees are common in Kenya's coastal areas, while acacia trees grow in the desert.

Climate

Kenya has a varied climate. The coastal climate is tropical. It is hot and humid. It has plenty of rainfall. Inland, less rain falls. The climate there is arid and semiarid. The Chalbi Desert covers much of northern Kenya. Chalbi means "bare and salty" in the Oromo language. Oromo is spoken by people in the region.

Kenya's highlands are cooler. Lower temperatures and steady rains support forests. Trees such as evergreens and cedars grow.

Kenya has two seasons. October to March is a dry season. Winds from Arabia bring warm and dry air. These winds are called Kaskazi. From April to September, winds from the Indian Ocean bring cooler, wetter air.

Must-See Stop:
Masai Mara National Reserve

Kenya is famous for its wildlife. One of the best places to see it is Masai Mara National Reserve. It is in southwestern Kenya. Visitors can see lions, rhinos, elephants, and zebras. Huge herds of wildebeest roam the grasslands. Over 450 bird species live in the reserve. Nature walks, hot-air balloon rides, and photo safaris are all great ways to see the reserve.

Chapter 2

HISTORY AND GOVERNMENT

Kenya's history goes back a long time. In Kenya, scientists have found stone tools that date back a million years. Humans evolved from early hominids. Scientists have found bones of early hominids that are six million years old!

Modern Humans

The earliest humans in Kenya were likely hunter-gatherers. Hunter-gatherers searched for their food.

They were always on the move. One of the first known cultures in Kenya were the Khoisan. Over the centuries, migration brought many new people. In the first century CE, Arab traders and Bantu-speaking people arrived. Sometimes, groups worked together. Other times, they fought for land and resources. Fighting between some of these groups still happens.

This skull found in Kenya could be 1.9 million years old.

Foreign Rule

In 1498, explorers from Portugal landed on Kenya's coast. They took over. Later, new empires controlled Kenya. The Omani Empire took power in 1698. The British Empire took over in 1895.

Kenya's people suffered under foreign rule. The land was stolen. Until the British ruled, people were captured. Some were sold into slavery. The traditions and cultures of native Kenyans were oppressed. People were forced to abandon their religions. They had to adopt Christianity or Islam.

Portuguese explorer Vasco da Gama arrived in Kenya in 1498.

THEN US PRESIDENT BARACK OBAMA ATTENDS
A NEWS CONFERENCE IN KENYA WITH KENYAN
PRESIDENT UHURU KENYATTA IN 2015.

Government

The Republic of Kenya has forty-seven counties. Each
county has a local government. The national government
has three branches. They are the legislative, executive,
and judicial branches.

The legislative branch is in charge of making laws. It is made up of the Senate and the National Assembly. The representatives work for these lawmaking bodies.

From left to right: **Then US secretary of state John Kerry and Kenyan president Uhuru Kenyatta meet at the State House in Nairobi, Kenya, in 2016.**

Let's Celebrate:
Madaraka Day!

Kenya's independence day is June 1. Kenyans gather for military parades. Singers and dancers entertain large crowds. For many, the highlight is a speech by Kenya's president. The president talks about Kenya's struggles for independence and the nation's future. The celebration ends with the singing of Kenya's national anthem.

The executive branch is led by the president of Kenya. This branch is in charge of enforcing laws.

The judicial branch applies the law. Kenya's highest court is the Supreme Court. The chief justice leads the Supreme Court.

THE STATE HOUSE IS THE OFFICIAL RESIDENCE OF THE PRESIDENT OF KENYA.

Chapter 3

CULTURE AND PEOPLE

Kenya is a nation of diversity. It is home to more than seventy ethnic groups. The largest group is the Kikuyu. They make up 17 percent of the population. Other big groups include the Luhya (14 percent), Kalenjin (13 percent), Luo (11 percent), and Kamba (10 percent). The smallest ethnic group is the El Molo, at about five hundred people.

Roman Catholic
children take part in
a religious event.

Religion

Kenya's constitution gives its people freedom of religion.
About 85 percent of Kenyans are Christian. And 11
percent are Muslim. Many Kenyans also practice a
variety of African religions. Sometimes people combine
these traditional beliefs with Christianity or Islam. They
create unique syncretic faiths. These faiths blend parts
of different religions. About 2 percent of Kenyans do not
practice a religion.

Language and Writing

Kenya has two official languages. They are English and Swahili. Its people also speak a wide range of African languages. These languages fall into three broad language families. The largest is Bantu. Bantu includes Swahili. Other languages are in the Nilotic and Cushitic families. Many Kenyans speak more than one language.

Swahili can be written in Arabic script. But the Latin alphabet is more commonly used.

A child attends a Swahili language class in Kenya.

Food and Art

Kenya blends a wide range of cuisines. Different ethnic groups cook in unique ways. Most of Kenya's food is based on grains. Corn, millet, and sorghum are all staples. A popular dish throughout Kenya is ugali. The porridge is made from corn flour or other grains. Nyama choma is grilled meat, often sheep or goat. Bean stews or shredded greens are often side dishes.

Kenya has a vibrant culture of arts, crafts, and music. Bright paintings often show natural scenes and wildlife. Some Kenyans craft ornate beaded necklaces. Some carve wooden figurines. Many Kenyans dance to up-tempo Benga music. Sigana is a type of performance art. It includes a lot of audience participation. And it combines storytelling, music, and dance.

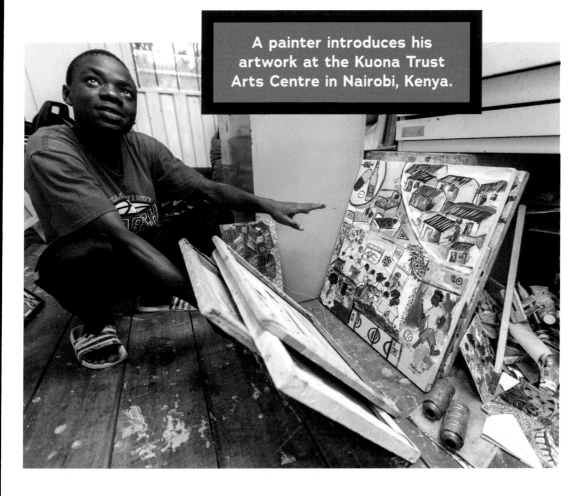

A painter introduces his artwork at the Kuona Trust Arts Centre in Nairobi, Kenya.

Must-See Stop:
Nairobi National Museum

Visitors can experience Kenya's culture and heritage at the Nairobi National Museum. It features traditional and modern works of Kenyan art. Here, people can see artifacts of Kenyan culture. They can see its gardens and learn more about the nation's history.

Chapter 4

DAILY LIFE

Kenya is home to about 54 million people. It is the world's twenty-seventh most populated nation. Many people live in small towns and rural areas. Only 27 percent of the population lives in urban areas. Nairobi is Kenya's largest city. It is home to 2.7 million people. Mombasa is the second largest, with about 800,000 people. Kenya's other cities are much smaller.

More than a third of Kenya's people have incomes below the poverty line. They work hard to provide for their households. About half work on small family farms. Crops include potatoes, corn, and sugarcane. Most children attend school, but many do not complete high school and instead take jobs to support their families.

A Kenyan woman works on her farm.

Let's Celebrate!
Lamu Cultural Festival

Lamu Island is party central each November. The island hosts the Lamu Cultural Festival. It celebrates Kenya's cultural roots. Events focus on traditional parts of Kenyan life. Visitors can take part in them. There are donkey races and Swahili poetry contests. Bao, an ancient board game, is played. People can enjoy shopping and learning about Kenyan culture.

The Future

Kenya is a growing nation. But it faces many challenges. These include health challenges such as malaria and tuberculosis. Many households also don't have access to healthful foods or clean water. Planning for the future can be difficult due to economic barriers.

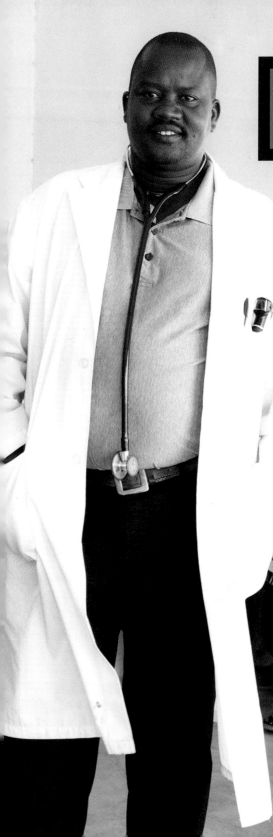

A doctor and patients in the waiting room at a rural Kenyan hospital

Yet Kenya's young people believe that conditions will improve. They understand the nation's many challenges, but they are eager to build a bright future.

A CLASSROOM IN RURAL KENYA
▼

Map and Key Facts

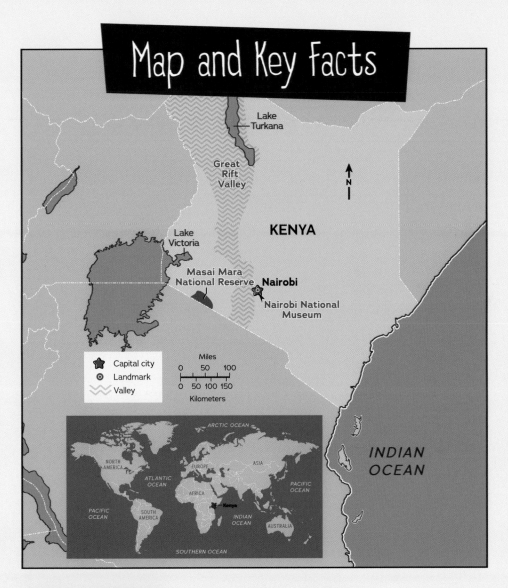

Lake Turkana

Great Rift Valley

Lake Victoria

KENYA

N

Masai Mara National Reserve

Nairobi

Nairobi National Museum

★ Capital city
◎ Landmark
〰 Valley

Miles
0   50   100

0 50 100 150
Kilometers

ARCTIC OCEAN

NORTH AMERICA

ATLANTIC OCEAN

EUROPE

ASIA

AFRICA

PACIFIC OCEAN

PACIFIC OCEAN

SOUTH AMERICA

INDIAN OCEAN

Kenya

AUSTRALIA

SOUTHERN OCEAN

INDIAN OCEAN

Flag of Kenya

- **Continent: Africa**
- **Capital city: Nairobi**
- **Population: 54 million**
- **Languages: English, Swahili, at least seventy other tribal languages and dialects**

Glossary

arid: having little or no rain

executive: the branch of a government responsible for putting laws into effect

hominid: a group of primates that includes humans and their distant ancestors

judicial: the branch of government responsible for interpreting laws

legislative: the lawmaking branch of government

plateau: a region of high, mostly level ground

syncretic faith: a religious belief that blends parts of two or more separate religions

tectonic plates: large masses of land that travel independently over Earth's mantle

tropical: a warm, humid climate found near Earth's equator

Learn More

Britannica Kids: Kenya
   https://kids.britannica.com/students/article/Kenya/275253

Edgar, Sherra G. *Kenya*. North Mankato, MN: Child's World, 2016.

Facts about Kenya
   https://www.kids-world-travel-guide.com/facts-about-kenya.html

Markovics, Joyce L. *Kenya*. New York: Bearport, 2019.

National Geographic Kids: Kenya
   https://kids.nationalgeographic.com/geography/countries/article
   /kenya

Rechner, Amy. *Kenya*. Minneapolis: Bellwether Media, 2019.

Index

Photo Acknowledgments

Image credits: Ninara/flickr (CC BY 2.0), p. 5; Sloot/iStock/Getty Images, p. 6; Gioia Forster/ picture-alliance/dpa/AP Images, p. 7; erichon/Shutterstock.com, p. 8 (left); © Santiago Urquijo/ Moment Open/Getty Images, p. 8 (right); Wajahat Mahmood/flickr (CC BY-SA 2.0), p. 9; Marion Kaplan/Alamy Stock Photo, p. 11; Sailko/Wikimedia Commons (CC BY 3.0), p. 12; REUTERS/Jonathan Ernst/Alamy Stock Photo, p. 13; U.S. Department of State/flickr, p. 14; YASUYOSHI CHIBA/AFP via Getty Images, p. 15; Maria Swärd/Moment/Getty Images, p. 16; Nicolas Marino/mauritius images GmbH/Alamy Stock Photo, p. 18; Bartosz Hadyniak/E+/Getty Images, p. 19; Mvuli-Girl/Wikimedia Commons (CC BY-SA 4.0), p. 20; Wang Teng/Xinhua/Alamy Stock Photo, p. 21; Images of Africa Photobank/Alamy Stock Photo, p. 22; The Sanitation and Hygiene Fund/flickr (CC BY 2.0), p. 24; Felix Masi/Africa Media Online/Alamy Stock Photo, p. 25; Hugh Sitton/Stone/Getty Images, pp. 27, 28; Laura K. Westlund, p. 29.

Cover: Devgnor/Moment/Getty Images.